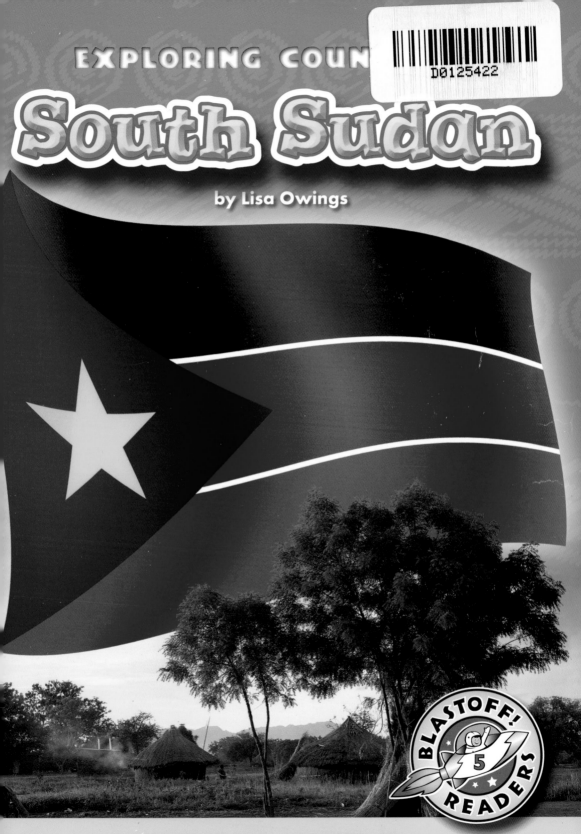

EXPLORING COUN

South Sudan

by Lisa Owings

BLASTOFF!
5
READERS

BELLWETHER MEDIA · MINNEAPOLIS, MN

Note to Librarians, Teachers, and Parents:

Blastoff! Readers are carefully developed by literacy experts and combine standards-based content with developmentally appropriate text.

Level 1 provides the most support through repetition of high-frequency words, light text, predictable sentence patterns, and strong visual support.

Level 2 offers early readers a bit more challenge through varied simple sentences, increased text load, and less repetition of high-frequency words.

Level 3 advances early-fluent readers toward fluency through increased text and concept load, less reliance on visuals, longer sentences, and more literary language.

Level 4 builds reading stamina by providing more text per page, increased use of punctuation, greater variation in sentence patterns, and increasingly challenging vocabulary.

Level 5 encourages children to move from "learning to read" to "reading to learn" by providing even more text, varied writing styles, and less familiar topics.

Whichever book is right for your reader, Blastoff! Readers are the perfect books to build confidence and encourage a love of reading that will last a lifetime!

This edition first published in 2013 by Bellwether Media, Inc.

No part of this publication may be reproduced in whole or in part without written permission of the publisher. For information regarding permission, write to Bellwether Media, Inc., Attention: Permissions Department, 5357 Penn Avenue South, Minneapolis, MN 55419.

Library of Congress Cataloging-in-Publication Data
Owings, Lisa.
 South Sudan / by Lisa Owings.
   p. cm. – (Blastoff! readers: exploring countries)
 Summary: "Developed by literacy experts for students in grades three through seven, this book introduces young readers to the geography and culture of South Sudan"–Provided by publisher.
 Includes bibliographical references and index.
 ISBN 978-1-60014-765-4 (hardcover : alk. paper)
 1. South Sudan–Maps. 2. South Sudan–Juvenile literature. I. Title. II. Series: Blastoff! readers. 5, Exploring countries.
 G2499.3.O9 2012
 962.9–dc23   2012007878

Printed in the United States of America, North Mankato, MN.

Contents

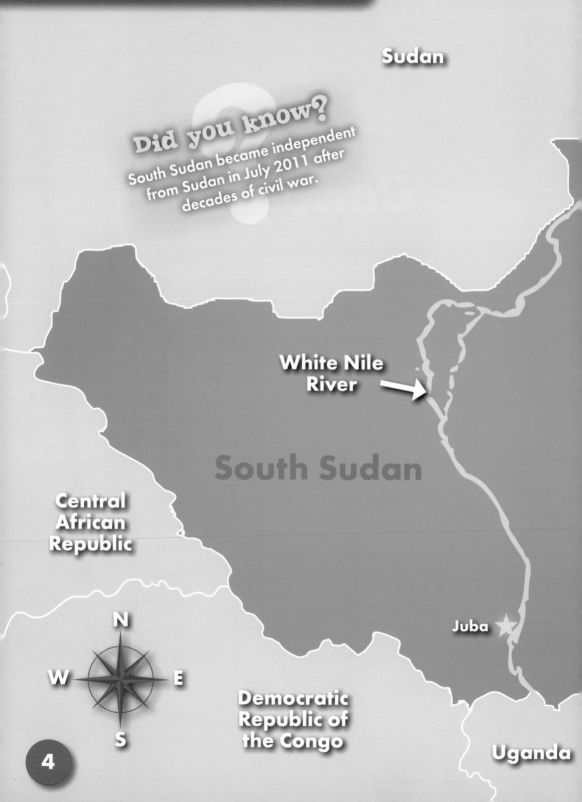

Sudan

Did you know?
South Sudan became independent from Sudan in July 2011 after decades of civil war.

White Nile River

South Sudan

Central African Republic

Democratic Republic of the Congo

Juba

Uganda

N
W   E
S

Ethiopia

Kenya

South Sudan became the world's newest country in 2011. It covers about 250,000 square miles (650,000 square kilometers) of eastern Africa. Sudan is its neighbor to the north, and Ethiopia lies to the east. South Sudan shares its southern border with Kenya, Uganda, and the Democratic Republic of the Congo. To the west is the Central African Republic.

South Sudan is **landlocked**. Its main source of water is the White Nile River. On the banks of this river is the country's capital city, Juba.

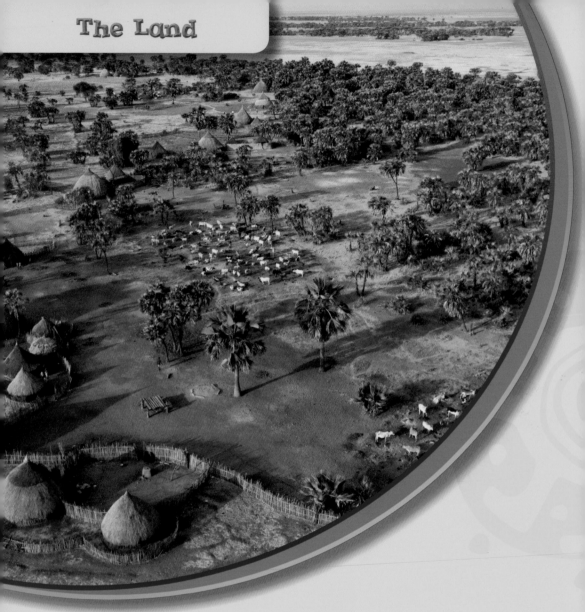

Thorny trees dot dry **savannahs** in much of South Sudan. Rivers and rainwater feed lush grasslands and wetlands in the center of the country. Mountains and hills are scattered along the country's edges. The Ironstone **Plateau** lies on the country's western border. The tall Imatong and Dongotona Mountains rise near the border with Uganda.

The White Nile flows into the country through the mountains and **rain forests** in the south. It passes through Juba on its way north. In the middle of the country, the river widens into a vast **swamp** called the Sudd. The weather in South Sudan is always warm. Rain comes during the wet season between April and December.

! fun fact

The Sudd is one of the world's largest swamps. It is an important habitat for the rare Nile lechwe antelope and the shoebill stork.

The Boma-Jonglei landscape stretches across eastern South Sudan. It is the largest grassland in East Africa. Herds of elephants, giraffes, and other African wildlife move across this region. Boma-Jonglei is also the location of one of the world's largest animal **migrations**.

Each year, the plains of South Sudan come alive. More than one million antelope leap across the landscape in search of food and water. White-eared kob, tiang, and other types of antelope make up these traveling herds. They move north toward the Sudd during the dry season. Later in the year, they follow the rains south. The leaders of South Sudan are working to protect the antelope and other animals. They hope their wealth of wildlife will draw people to the country from all over the world.

Did you know?
Many experts believe the wildlife migration in South Sudan is the second largest in the world.

giant eland

Nile perch

Did you know?

The rare giant eland can be spotted in South Sudan. This huge antelope can weigh up to 2,000 pounds (900 kilograms). Its horns can reach 4 feet (1.2 meters) long!

cheetah

Many large African **mammals** roam across South Sudan. Groups of elephants and hippopotamuses gather in the Sudd. Lions, leopards, and cheetahs hide in tall grasses. They wait for zebras, giraffes, and buffalo to wander from their herds. Antelope bound across the plains.

Nile crocodile

Rain forest **canopies** shelter chimpanzees and baboons. Ostriches race across the savannahs. The country's swamps are home to storks, pelicans, and cranes. Nile crocodiles wait in rivers for prey to take a drink. They share their homes with Nile perch. These giant fish can grow to be more than 300 pounds (140 kilograms)!

Did you know?

Around 27,000 Sudanese boys were separated from their families during the war. They formed a group and walked hundreds of miles to the safety of neighboring countries. Many have found their families again.

More than 10.5 million people live in South Sudan. Most of them are **native** to Africa. Some Arabs also live in the country. The Dinka are the largest group of South Sudanese. They share the land with the Nuer, Shilluk, and many smaller groups. South Sudan also provides shelter for **refugees** from Sudan and other countries.

English and Arabic are the official languages of South Sudan. Many people groups also speak their own languages. Most South Sudanese are Christian or follow **animist** religions. Families and communities have close relationships. Most people are friendly and generous.

Speak Arabic!

The South Sudanese use Arabic script when they write. However, Arabic words can be written in English to help you read them out loud.

English	Arabic	How to say it
hello	salaam	sah-LAHM
good-bye	ma'as salaama	MA-as sa-LAH-mah
yes	aywa	EYE-wuh
no	la	lah
please	min fadlak	min FAD-lahk
thank you	shukran	SHOO-kran
friend (male)	sadīq	sah-DEEK
friend (female)	sadīqa	sah-DEEK-ah

Most South Sudanese live in the countryside. Their villages are clustered near rivers. They build **traditional** houses called *tukuls* out of mud and grass. Families work together to raise enough crops or livestock to live on. Children help with daily chores such as fetching water and grinding grains. Most people walk to get from place to place.

People in cities live in apartments, small houses, or tents. They have better access to food, clean water, electricity, and healthcare than those in the countryside. Life can be difficult in South Sudan. The war that led to the country's independence caused much damage. The South Sudanese are working hard to improve their living conditions.

Where People Live in South Sudan

cities
22%

countryside
78%

fun fact

There are about as many cows as there are people in South Sudan. People often trade cattle instead of money to buy goods.

Many children were not able to go to school during the war. It was too dangerous. Today, about half of the children in South Sudan attend primary school. Starting at age 6, they learn to read, write, and speak English. They also learn about art, math, and the environment. After eight years of primary school, few students move on to secondary school. Graduates can attend one of South Sudan's recently reopened universities. The schools were closed or relocated during the war.

The South Sudanese plan to build more schools. They also need more teachers and school supplies. They hope one day all children will be able to attend school.

Did you know?
Only about one out of every four South Sudanese adults can read and write.

17

Did you know?

South Sudan is rich in oil. However, it needs Sudan's help to process and sell the oil. The two countries are struggling to agree on how to share this resource.

Most South Sudanese are farmers. They grow **sorghum**, corn, and rice in the rich soils near the White Nile. Dinka and Nuer families care for large herds of cattle. Others raise sheep or goats. Many farmers produce just enough to feed their families. Some sell their products in local markets.

South Sudan is rich in **natural resources**. Wood, nuts, and other resources are harvested from its forests. Fish are caught in its rivers. Many workers bring up oil from underground. This is the country's most important resource. Many South Sudanese are moving to cities to work in schools or hospitals. Some also run small businesses.

The South Sudanese love to sing and dance. Music brings them together to celebrate important events. They also use song and dance to cheer for sports teams. Wrestling and basketball are favorite sports. A few South Sudanese basketball players are known around the world for their talent. Soccer has also become popular.

In their free time, families cool off in the country's rivers. National parks offer hiking trails and the chance to see a variety of wildlife. In the evenings, children gather to listen to stories or play outside with friends. When it is very hot, families listen to the radio or watch television indoors.

fun fact

Famous United States basketball player Manute Bol was from southern Sudan. At 7 feet 7 inches (2.3 meters), he was one of the tallest players in the NBA.

sorghum

Rich soil provides South Sudanese with a variety of grains, vegetables, and fruits. Fish is popular in river communities. Those who raise livestock eat more beef, lamb, and milk. Stew and **porridge** are common across the country. *Ful* is a traditional stew of mashed fava beans and spices. Sorghum porridge called *asida* is often served with meat or vegetables. *Kisra* is a flatbread eaten with most meals.

Many South Sudanese eat two meals a day. They drink tea before going to work or school. Then they come home for lunch, the main meal of the day. Dinner is usually light. Bananas, papayas, and mangoes are sweet snacks.

fun fact

Karkadé is a popular South Sudanese beverage. This deep red tea gets its color from hibiscus flowers.

karkadé

ful

kisra

South Sudanese look forward to several national holidays. They celebrated their first Independence Day on July 9, 2011. People across the nation gathered to cheer, dance, and wave their country's new flag. On July 30, people light candles to honor those who died fighting for South Sudan. The country's leaders give speeches in their memory.

Christians in South Sudan celebrate Christmas in December. Many decorate their homes. Family and friends gather inside. They feast on meat dishes and pray together. Some families exchange gifts.

Christmas

fun fact

After the peace agreement in 2005, southern Sudanese had six years to decide if they wanted independence. In 2011, nearly every person voted in favor of independence.

Southern Sudan was at war with northern Sudan for about 50 years. The northern Sudanese controlled the government. They wanted those in the south to follow their laws and beliefs. The southern Sudanese fought to keep their culture. War raged between the groups until 2005. Millions of people died or lost their homes.

The South Sudanese have much to celebrate now that they are free and independent. However, they also face many challenges. They must establish a government to meet the needs of the people. New schools, hospitals, and roads must be built. The South Sudanese are hopeful that with help from other nations, they can build a beautiful country.

Fast Facts About South Sudan

South Sudan's Flag

The flag of South Sudan has three horizontal bands of black, red, and green. These bands are separated by thin white stripes. The left side of the flag features a blue triangle with a yellow star in its center. The black band represents the African people. Red stands for sacrifice, and white stands for peace. The land of South Sudan and the waters of the Nile inspired the green and blue colors. The star stands for unity and hope.

Official Name: Republic of South Sudan

Area: 248,777 square miles
(644,329 square kilometers);
South Sudan is the 42nd largest
country in the world.

Capital City:	Juba
Important Cities:	Malakal, Wau, Yei
Population:	10,625,176 (July 2012)
Official Languages:	English, Arabic
National Holiday:	Independence Day (July 9)
Religions:	animist, Christian, Muslim
Major Industries:	farming, fuel
Natural Resources:	farmland, fish, oil, gold, diamonds, timber, iron ore, copper, silver
Manufactured Products:	food products, building materials
Farm Products:	sorghum, corn, rice, wheat, sugarcane, mangoes, papayas, bananas, cotton, sweet potatoes, cassava, peanuts, cattle, sheep
Unit of Money:	South Sudanese pound; the pound is divided into 100 piastres.

Glossary

animist—based in nature and the belief that spirits exist in the natural environment

canopies—thick coverings of leafy branches in rain forests; canopies are formed by the tops of trees.

landlocked—completely surrounded by land

mammals—animals that have hair and produce milk to feed their young

migrations—events in which animals move from one place to another; animals usually migrate to find food or a safe place to raise their young.

native—originally from a specific place

natural resources—materials in the earth that are taken out and used to make products or fuel

plateau—an area of flat, raised land

porridge—hot cereal made by boiling grains in milk or water

rain forests—dense tropical forests where rain falls most of the year

refugees—people who were forced to leave their countries to escape war or natural disasters

savannahs—dry, grassy plains

sorghum—a type of grain that can be eaten or used as animal feed; sorghum is an important crop for the South Sudanese.

swamp—an area of land that is covered with water and green plants

traditional—relating to stories, beliefs, or ways of life that families or groups hand down from one generation to the next

To Learn More

AT THE LIBRARY

Burlingame, Jeff. *The Lost Boys of Sudan*. New York, N.Y.: Marshall Cavendish Benchmark, 2011.

Mead, Alice. *Year of No Rain*. New York, N.Y.: Farrar, Straus and Giroux, 2003.

Park, Linda Sue. *A Long Walk to Water*. Boston, Mass.: Clarion Books, 2010.

ON THE WEB

Learning more about South Sudan is as easy as 1, 2, 3.

1. Go to www.factsurfer.com.

2. Enter "South Sudan" into the search box.

3. Click the "Surf" button and you will see a list of related Web sites.

With factsurfer.com, finding more information is just a click away.

Index